C.S.U. Poetry Series XLIII

Claudia Keelan

REFINERY

Cleveland State University Poetry Center

ACKNOWLEDGMENTS

Grateful acknowledgment is made to the following publications, in which poems from *Refinery* first appeared:

Black Warrior Review: "Angel Wing"
Calliope: "Refinery," "Romanticism"
Denver Quarterly: "Lines Where the Fence Is Crossed," "If Not in the Field Then Where"
Indiana Review: "Indian Paint Brush," "Mid, Mid-West"
Ironwood: "Love as the Dirt of History"
Pequod: "To My Teacher"
Poetry Flash: "Shanti Town"
Ploughshares: "Towards"
Sonora Review: "Icarus' Remembered Anatomy," "Sundial," "Teaching Tragedy"
South Florida Review: "Poem for the Closing of the Last Leper Colony," "Ars Poetica"
Southern Poetry Review: "No Excuses"
The Taos Review: "Suicide with an Ocean View," "Winter Palm," "Where the Train Meets the River"

Thanks go to the Helene Wurlitzer Foundation, especially to Henry, whose combativeness helped immensely.

Funded Through
Ohio Arts Council

CONTENTS

To my mother and father,
and with special thanks
to Winifred Gegan.

I. The Sun

NO EXCUSES

The grass is wild.
It starts like that.
The teeth then and the meadow
of hair at your neck and then:
the gun is wild.

                    The coyotes trailed the
long tractor mowing the hay for winter. The blades
churned the field mice up in its wake, into the
mouths of the waiting dogs. The blades were the sun
for both planets, mouse and dog.

This story is not mine and the sun reflected
on the clay road there is wild. The tree thickets
are wild. The sun in the blades of grass
in the meadow is not mine but see how I live in the air,
all three—tractor, mice, hungry dogs—travel, doing
my job, tearing through notions of grass
and flesh to make sense of the embarrassing,
unrestrained sky. The sun pours down like rain

on the wild underbrush near the edge
of remorse, the closest town,
where the deputy has just killed
the innocent fugitive with one shot.
His dull slug jails me in the barred back seat
of the present: almost servile, this contrived
instinct gulps water sniffed out by my dearest
enemy: I lie down and reason rifles my hair.

TEACHING TRAGEDY

Because the day includes
the repetitious noise
of school children caught
in a whirlpool, the downward
motion and hiss signaling
something I can't remember
or don't know and the sun's
latent promise, another back
against whose wall . . .
I wish I could break
into flames for you
while saying *the hero,*
when he dies, is cleansed,
and something is returned
to us and lay my prophetic
hand on your arm.
The day is madness,
including the beginning
which promises sight,
the middle eclipsed
by persistence, our blood
in a sieve, and the end
which asks for more
than an explanation
and the heart trapped
in the throat. I keep
forgetting what I want
to say, but it's a day, it's only
a day. It's as if all that existed
before the moment your name
went down in the Bureau of Vital
Statistics was the unbroken
summer air, before the locust
came and swallowed the tree entire.

WINTER PALM

I only love what I don't
        have, the sun too feeble

to make an appearance, a body
        I hold and burn, remembering,

shadow its gift the electric
        wire sways back and forth

in the tedious, blue day room.
        What I wouldn't give

for the random bright spots
        this light makes of cesspools,

resting on a muddy rim, to see right
        the floating doll's head, the dead

we love, onward in the pool, mouthing
        still "I'm blind, don't you see

I can't die without you?"
        Love, come back to me.

The trees' arms are breaking
        without you. The weak

impressions the alders make
        against a brick wall

deflect the spark you say you see
        when you look into my eyes.

I'll give you a dollar for that
        ashtray, the postcard from Peoria.

I love memorabilia from a past
        I don't belong to.

There's no marquee for you to fall
        from. There never was.

SHANTI TOWN

> "What place is this, what country,
> what region of the world?"
> —Seneca, *Hercules Furens*

Yet how is it everything
has its day with me?
A mongoloid on a bicycle
wants peace in the world.
His tee shirt bears the Japanese
symbol for tranquility
as he pushes instead of pedals
intoning ah ah ah ah
down the rutted road.
He has not been reading Einstein
late into the nights
but if he had, a symphony
could blossom forth from
his chest, flutes prevailing
over the rumble of the bass,
trilling past the heads
of the audience to spill
sweetly into the street, a bird,
a survivor bird black with fatigue,
exiting the order of a music
too strident for the colorful
subtle shifts the trees
achieve of one motion. Poor bird,
see how she lives out of context,
the trees so late, too beyond
lush and plentiful for belief.
She wants to turn
back into music, refuse to land,
live as a trembling suspended
over our heads forever.
How is it they continue
to kill their children, poor

illiterate paragons, taking
a bite before they offer
a tithe to the state? Oh bird,
what you hear is the songs
of the war *between*
any single land, a yammering
inside the bones,
the parasite grown
accustomed to, the one
we weep to kill.

SANCTUARY

Miss World of 1939 is sad.
Alone in her art gallery
circa 1980, the winged
Indian man of god burns
flourescently in her honor.
Who will dare to let her make her bed?
The grey in her eyes curves
away from possession, living
somewhere so humid and dense,
those who left when she was
crowned have been years, and still
not found her, in the travel.
I want to protect Miss World,
take her away from these carnival
crucifixes, free her from yet
another grinning Nazi dinner
party, forever. Of herself
she says only "I knew, you see,
there was a needle in the skin
between my thumb and index
but I could not, no I
refused to open my eyes.
The doctor kept asking
are you angry, are you angry
but I had named that needle before
with my eyes closed." Her hands folded
into a temple in her lap. "You will
never know how sad." How many, dear
beauty, how many longed to crawl
to safety under those hands? Relics,
Miss World, in hissing human form,
of what we'd do to own you.

MEDEA

Because she loved too well,
Medea, to regain herself,
killed her children
and cutting her brother's body
into pieces, threw them easily
over the water. Suspended,
their reflection—eye into knee,
breast hinged to lip, curve
of thigh joining the fine blade
his shoulder had once been—
he became whole once
before cloth-like he unfolded,
descending into the water
like a carpet thrown to hide
some white, telling scar.
I want to say
that loss is a matter of not knowing
when to stop,
when to shred yourself
back into yourself,
the uprooting gained
defining at least some sliver
of bone and heart.
The sky at evening
holds within itself
relic fragments of light.
A skylark, unfolding,
appears suddenly—I want to see
how his eye catches the light,
how the night falls pretending
to be beautiful, how the bird,
suddenly blind, feels
the playing for keeps of it.
I can see their coming together—
earth, bird—but what it feels like
is descent, the desire
to be grounded, the emphasis
put on arrival and departure.

ROMANTICISM

It is not the clay road
on which a woman travels
clutching a baby in one arm
and holding an older boy's hand
while he eats an apple.
I think it must be
in what the boy sees as he walks
there, caught in the sweetness
of apple, in the love it allows
him as he bites suddenly
his cheek, as he turns his face
up to his mother, wanting to cry
but stopping himself, *how tired
she is* and he has only just begun
to bleed. And it's how I want
to let him keep looking away
from her who has his hand,
at wild flowers, the old town,
anywhere but at his feet.

ICARUS' REMEMBERED ANATOMY

If he cried
when they killed each bird,
breaking the delicate
necks, fingers shaking
more with his wish
for the sun, with his desire
to live his idea and rise
innocent on contrived
wings into the air,
what more could he pay,
fleshed, mortal,
holding each body
up against the light,
illuminating for a moment
each fine line of bone
before he tore,
in praise of flight,
the ridges of feather
from their bodies?
He was already
suspended, stained
in precarious balance
between earth and sky,
his hands no longer
his own, bloody,
with the purpose of his idea.
He was already
so far gone, face threading
into the grey shelter
of the sky, what could matter,
the dark ground losing
definition, the mangled,
necessary bodies left
in the wake of his absence
and his need to remember.

DEATH OF THE OBJECT

1. Dachau

I recognize you by your shape.
Unimposing doorway, circa 1944,
just a visible space, waiting to be filled.
Who can blame your hunger?
The good son merely saying "after your shower,
father, then we will talk. . . . "
The old man swallowed
and the version of his face,
turning, in his son, back
to the day, sun flinching
against a hollow in his neck, not
afraid, yes, the smoke rising is almost relief.

2. Baptism

There's a rose at the feet
of the blessed Mary
locked in the rectory yard.
I think a priest put it there.
I think he loves Mary, even
though she's quite reserved
despite her arms that keep
spreading out to everyone.
It's not a sin to love
a piece of stone, is it?
It's less of a wrong
if she won't, indeed,
can't return his love, isn't it?
So he'll be forgiven his furtive
walk to her cold feet each day, won't he?
God forgive him if his prayers
are answered and she opens her mouth.

3. The California Theatre

It's harder to see this sidewalk
than your face as you fell
from the ladder. I wasn't there.
I think, though, that's when
you turned into an angel,
in the grace of that fall,
hair loosening into the near hysteria
of the evangelicals on the corner,
marquee light pulsing in a kind of
love . . . who would want to recover
after the beauty of that arc?
It was that pain you learned to honor,
the cry you didn't make
as you hit the cement,
the story I render
as I impose upon the day.

4.

Before the decline of an empire,
the heroes are replaced by stars.
The hero is eaten willingly
by the lion, the star dazzles
in his aluminum loin cloth,
the snaps he places accurately
to guide the lion's feet
grow beautiful in the shabbiness
of the hero's stumble.
The lion wants only
the poor man's liver,
the star, the glass rosary beads
shining around his waist. *But the ladies,
the gentlemen, my good audience?*
The shed petals
in the easiness of his defeat.

SONG

Because it's all I have to give.
The nerve strung across the city
has its moment: it flips on, blood
dried to a mere stain, flips off, who
has ever seen well enough? But it's not nerve
I need, not now. I want to brighten slowly,
small star, solitary but not indifferent
above the one or two eyes raised tonight.
I want to be the eyes. City,
$\qquad$ I don't know you,
mired as you are in the river,
will you open your doors to the rower
who glides by, no place to go
but on? The lights are muted there, I know,
and the people looking through the cafe window
aren't even looking for something to eat. Famished.
I'm famished. Forgive them, forgive me.
We would begin again if we could,
allow the trees their shed skin
without envy, hold dirt and leaves to our bodies
for a different reason than shame.
We'd be lying to say we're sorry
we wanted, I'd be lying to say
this is enough, clenched as I am
in the light of these bridge flares
tonight, wanting something else,
anything else than the gnarl of stars
and buildings that yammer *god, man, god, man . . .*
into the same air the rower pulls
both god and man
and he doesn't even know it.

II. The Tree

TWO AUTOBIOGRAPHIES

1. Narcissus

Let the clandestine hollow where they will, I go where I'm invited.

My father was a tool salesman when I was born, slam.

Hammer, rake, pitchfork, hoe he was thirty-five and thinking

"Hard metal," bent sure to his knees and praying for rain as he rose over my mother.

She was smiling, her face turned slightly to the side saying "garden, garden . . . "

She was longing to be a flower bulb, to bloom once and well, leaving a scent still suspended in the air.

I was left a tree, a wheel, and a scrap of song scarcely heard, "Give you a chance at me."

My guardian angel in the picture on the wall would save me, but I knew better; her dress was too blue.

My guardian angel hovered over a bridge where a small, blonde girl walked, holding a doll; neither wore an expression.

Below the bridge the water was dimly brown; the bridge collapsed.

I pulled my sheets around my neck listening for the moment the water slapped the land.

I saw no reason to talk about the temperature of the water when it was the close cornered sky I turned my face to.

2. The Image

I was there because I thought there would be more like me
there.

Nonetheless, I grew frightened at how I receded into
myself, mouth overtaking mouth, eye into eye, I blinked.

Beyond the black bank and willows fingering down, a
manmade pulley, a caught fish line, various small bursts of
color.

But there in the cool ripples, in water that could not go
deep enough, rocks grazed my hands, I was safe.

They were wrong. A man is an island and I am there; there
is light in black pockets, someone combs my hair.

I was no more part of the mud than a footprint, I was a
rock turned fossil, and imbedded, angry, angry.

Ships carrying delayed cargo went past and past, a
whirlpool of motion but no sure passage.

Someone surely could have raised a white flag then but it
was thought foolish to admit fear.

But they were boats at first, not ships, and wind filled the
sails, there was food for a lifetime.

And no one liked the food from the start, not the clown, or
the ladies, or the little prince.

Someone called the police but they were out subduing the
firstborn.

When the commander-in-chief realized he'd slain his only
son, he fell with a strangled cry.

In general, I was a military type and had to dive in or
drown.

SUNDIAL

It is deafening
where the past lives.
At the doorway
light diminishes
and the lanterns hiss.
Aspen stand in between
all the different pines
and the browning cones
break underfoot. Listening
inside their cocoons,
the growing larvae wait
and someone stops breathing.
To explain the time I make
for time to inhabit me
I speak of weather but weather
is only the second hand.
You can see the minutes part
as though looking into your parent's
grave with a child, hand in hand.
The past is lost there,
All the parts you remember.

MID, MID-WEST

The sun continues to burn behind the eyes
and a song, something about grace and one
you've loved for years, sounds a lie,
tinny now. The dirt can't contain this, the dirt
doesn't know how. And so your face is found,
all of it, mouth opened, waiting for rain. It was
lost for years in a disdain, hard worked for.
Somehow it's still not believable but it's all you
can do. The orders only said march, and the day not
asked for. What to do? In the field a farmer
crumples paper into the dirt. The harvest is
planned and nothing can stop it, now that you're
this far from home: gold-rimmed in the rear view
mirror *take me back* you cried.

INDIAN PAINT BRUSH

Placed now between the pages, the fire
I brought back is ebbing. Sorrow is a lot
the neon weed flickered in, once
the old man's narrow alley
became, finally, his.

The porch door hanging by one broken hinge
flies further open. Twisted
by you and every wind, welcome
was its only word and the solitary
flute barely heard in the near dead

Summer plays beyond these children's
good night screams. Sometimes it's necessary
to stop listening in order to hear.
Once I wanted in
but now that I find myself here

I wish I was smoke.

TEACHING BRAILLE

Sun half way down the building
navigates the grained surface.

It wants to keep a coup de grace
with me, but you (the undermining

of crocus, snow frozen to a grey mountain
in the street, all my resistance),

graceless listener, in your headset
the announcer is mouthing

sound for the end of the world.
We're both the same. I try to love you

but you interrupt. Your voice breaks
in the lock. Will you take the spring away, too?

THE SUNFLOWER

Rearing your head once
in the scrap of dirt
between clapboard houses—

    Evangelical flower,
the monotone of your rising
clacks on. Tending
(what else to do with this history's
dirt but let it pass through
your hands, glad for the stain, glad)

    all the old
believers flame out
with you, yellow scream,
failing in refinery smoke,
in the used up skyline,
for what?

    We can't muster
(these streets the catacomb,
these children the muted)
your frenzy, nursing sterility
in an old city's time.

    Behold the day savaged
on the periphery of the sidewalks,
my smell joining other food smells,
face reflecting in the store window
takes its place on the confectioner's

    shelf, and made to!
for the browsers binging in the aisle.
Dread now, my only love,

the scarred face mumbling in the olive
aisle asks for high poetry.

    Nothing I say
places her within reach.

WHERE THE TRAIN MEETS THE RIVER

Believe me, I wanted
                the reply my life
couldn't smear the tracings
                of in the rain's low
voweled madness against the train
                window. I was falling
in that reflected downpour, trees' arms
                skeletal in the excess space
the sky fakes, my twice removed blood,
                my parenthetical bond,
finally only the sudden catch the Charles River
                gleaned in my throat
after the darkness of the tunnel. Only a moment,
                only a moment was my life
removed from the face I looked away from
                in the window. I wanted to be on
the train. I wanted to be more than reflection.
                I wanted to put my fingers
into the mouth of the baby's scream ricocheting
                in the suddenly quiet car,
but the gathering roar works as a buffer
                to infant trauma as if anything
so loud, so deafening, must be god,
                so instinctively baby stops
to listen. It's mother's *shh, shh* taking form
                in the train's gaining momentum,
the whispered lullabies for extinction.
                Believe me, I'm speaking
trying to monitor this breathing—it must be
                breathing—inhaling the part
of me that wants to look away. What then,
                and whom, has turned my face to
rain?

LINES THAT RELY ON VOICE FOR AUTHENTICITY

> . . . and even now I cannot be sure the words
> I speak are my own, but some soul who has
> inhabited my spirit.
>
> —Keats

Because the dark streaks the day left
are not just the last claw mark
of an envious sun but a dirt
I feel smeared all over my face,
and the mother of god's confinement
in an endless series of boxes strewn
all over this neighborhood seems a fitting place
for yet another fin de siècle of reverence,
a hallowed ground for the crazy, broken believer
pinioned raving on his front porch
where he must look to the lord god brick wall
for solace, inconsolable. The breath of smoke
this train expels goes a long way back.
The animal next door
is a broken animal.
I can barely see him, how will I love him?

He is my neighbor,
for the love of whom, he is my neighbor.
I marvel in my daily faith,
ascending onto the train's platform and into
the crowded car, assuming I will arrive
intact, a perfect bit of cloth and flesh,
a memento. I find myself mouthing
*it was the best of times, it was the worst
of times,* and I am stuck,
best languishing in the slow decay
of the last summer flower down the street.
I am speaking in a voice that is not now, or ever,
mine. The air clenching around my face
is dictated by a wind of amnesia, a history

of *cleave and you will be* . . . a rape I was witness
to, but drove by, afraid to stop
to see the damage for sure.

Because to see it
would be to see
his pitiful stoop for what it is,
a shitting place for pigeons,
a bad place to die.

And we're only going to work,
sure that the black tunnel will emerge
into the first mirage
this day seems to offer,
in which all this commerce and religion
will grow, in the razed skyline,
suddenly beautiful.

This air not quite thick enough to drown out his
screams, not quite thick enough to let the words I
need squeeze through, but I've not yet fallen
to my knees, and I'm not so sure
broken animal's quite broken, refusing
to muster in this kind of air.

To muster in this kind of air,
for the love of you, godless
god of the father, this poetry
of fiction and dull strife
that will not harm, nor save you?

In my heart, the buds of thousands of small desert
flowers burn to flourish. They will flourish
for you, lord reader, for you,
broken animal. If I could
cease in ceasing,
in my unceasing love for you,
silent man, win or take all the winner
of this duel, the one where the right
word could have saved you.

WHERE THE ELECTRIC WIRES DISAPPEAR FROM VIEW

Plant something true for me.
New shoes or a wool sweater,
the arms folded into each other.
Directed by their buzz,
I'll be clothed at least.
Oh Nebraska as I've never known you

what let you lie down so completely?
Your open fields promised China
at least, in their unseen end, the scarecrow,
ragged liar, once and for all
consumed by flames, the sun finally slipping
through without flattening.

Where the electric wires disappear from view,
your ranging grass turns the corner at last:
Wanderer, it was merely a 90 degree angle
your body travelled, until you got spooked
and hurried back, wiping mud from your feet,
to join the one who never imagined such freedom,
asleep on her back with her mouth open.

POEM AT THE CLOSING OF THE LAST LEPER COLONY

for Maria Gonzalez

"A wingless song,
she is most like the birds
they shoot in countries
other than this. Here
we put them in cages
in Woolworth's and how they
shriek to each other
without stop, or until
they stop which means
a purple eye closes and feathers
grow dim one by one
and in a solidarity of the dying
they drop together, bright
spots lying still on the black words."

IF NOT IN THE FIELD THEN WHERE

The first of October and still
the insects deliver prayers in an idiom not understood
but for the emphasis, can you hear it, on finish. All summer
their large republic, unholy choir, punctuated
the actions of things until it was impossible
to live here without them. That music everywhere so that
even the littlest boys fumbled catches in the baseball field,
their parents' digressive troubled love, *that's my boy*
seemed rote, orchestrated. And then the falling down
of days, deals in car lots, the order of the church bell,
rubble, rubble. I tried to catch one today, cicada, good
word. I even had a glass jar. I walked the periphery of the
town, I stood on the edge of a far field. I entered the field.
I got down on my knees, I crawled, jar in my mouth. I peeled
the brown leaves of corn, looked for it in the fruit.
If not in the field then where, and I'm stroking
the unseen, following their directive to its very edge: not in
the trees, but *in* them, not on the road, but by it, not in this
listening, but through it. Here? In the neighborhood's lie
of order, this promise among us? Here, teacher, in the headlights
in this stumbling travel, I am afraid
of the intermittent flashing of light that I must touch the body
of this sound in, because fingering these silken wings might still
it, my head uncovered, unprepared in earnest
for this snow I fall in.

III. The Sun in the Tree

REFINERY

Let the words fall, please just let them.
With all we've abandoned by now
chances are we could piece the fallen
city together by recall, assemble

the family members for a new portrait.
We could put the terror in reverse: how
the black chalk erases off the faces and the blood
returns from the salt water, filling

the scattered limbs that are assembling now,
back onto the bodies. How the boys, enamored,
amnesiac, stare down at their boots until

they board the ships and sail back the way
they came from, the sands left unstained,
apologies forgotten in their throats.

SUICIDE WITH AN OCEAN VIEW

1. Apollo

His idea was the sun brought up.

The light passed over some rocks,
a tenement, went through the slow
parting of a mourning curtain. It held. It had to

hold: *rock, tenement, grief.*
And if it wasn't love,
the shadows lay heavy on the ground, the passed-over
version of what is there.

"No speeches," he cried, swinging from power line
to power line, "order, you are my context. . . . "
The hard, hungry, and sad, all in their places.

2. Daphne

Alone to piece the past again,
she is either real sad
or real mean. The sun is out. The streets are dry.

The tree, rigid, was only a promise
he thought the day held, it had
to hold. The leaves sputter, laughing

against the sheer arrogance of the sun, or wind,
whatever elements they are that take away,
fade the green. She only knows his movement

across her (the light making its way between
two buildings now) his faith,
is her fault. The leaves too are cowards.

They turn yellow. They fall easily to the ground.

3. The Sun in the Tree

What is it like then, to be left
in the dullness of an in-between
season? And is it dullness

or dull hope before the final, well kept promise
that makes the leaves clench, not quite
ready to drop, inspires the sun, well

meaning, easing between the center
of it all? One bird calls, one
answers, a river's current moves

back and back against itself,
evening (this is evening, fear,
all desire a fear) laying down

its borders. The sun only wanted
the tree to bear witness, host
picnics, bear fine cloth slowly

draped against the trunk, spread
its arms to a light it knew
nothing of. The tree, rigid,

lived in a perpetual winter; prey
to no parasite, it is already
beyond cold; no thought lives

here, only form caught in a running
fright. It is winter. The tree is only
a cold thing the sun recites justice to.

LOVE AS THE DIRT OF HISTORY

There is a dirt spreading across the smiles
of the mercenary, the mercenary's whore,
pooling, in Golub's street scenes,
across sidewalks and hands
of bystanders, easing nearly off
the canvas itself, it is that alive.
In the same way, his Napalm Gate
unfastens from its pillar (this could be
the gate to heaven or hell, for all its shine,
this could be my way out
of the art museum), lending itself,
in other scenes, to replace an arm here,
consume the better half of this jungle there,
the larger part of this metallic arch
composing the smile in the dead
sergeant's face. What is the dirt
adorning these faces? The sum of a history
I was born into, so that even
while I leave this arena, walk past
and away from these ornate halls,
I feel it filming my eyes as I take in
the day . . . is it napalm closing my mouth
each time I dare to speak? Outside,
the vendor counts my change
slowly, the bus I need doesn't even slow
as it goes by. I contemplate my face
in an aluminum truck, and when he finds
I'm still there he asks "what more,"
as if I could tell him,
as if I couldn't see the sunlight (the necessary
metal, this soothing even as you burn)
glare until he averts his eyes.

* * * *

What goes around comes around
is a saying I've never understood
being how I am always where
you, or I, left me. Briefly, in spring,
the flowers gain dominance
over the yellow of the hills. Yet, in summer,
the yellow resumes its strain,
sliding across the refinery stacks and oil bins
until the flowers, loved once for the color
they gave, are remembered with hatred,
another promise sapped, broken.
Does that make it clearer? The flowers, I mean,
is it their absence we despise? Without them,
the dry grass is not a negotiable quality,
it is, merely dry. Try "Franco, alive, was terror,
easily understood, banal terror . . . " against
"dead, encased permanently in the silk coffin,
he lives like the stunted cancer . . . his profile
reproduced in wirephotos, in paintings,
is the hardened growth subdued,
that hidden, mysterious,
he will be impossible to forget . . . ."
I was trying to say I am the same here,
shuffling through the days,
cursing and praising the tree's strength
in the same breath, but I find I am not.
It is so cold it is hard to breathe
and the trees, therefore, are confusing,
just confusing. I'd like to say
I still love as I used to
but terror does something to the heart.

* * * *

Keens it? So that even the city's lack of brown
grass grows you, the sounds more animal than not
become more than a day, six months, 26 years
of omission. Being how I am always where
you or I left me, I am, briefly.
The trees extend their arms.
They reach over the fence, into a playground.
The trees extend their arms (as in a prayer?)
and I think that from either side
of this fence I could pull into the branches.
Though there are no leaves
to hide me from sight
I imagine the snow's whiteness
a camouflage, of sorts.

LINES WHERE THE FENCE IS CROSSED

Begin with *are you for me*
or against me, for me
or against
      A backdrop, that's all.
Any hero ragged,
      Any border owned
And only your dog or your tears to hold you up
—"right."

          * * * *

Bury my heart in me,
all's I ask.
There's an electric wire
round the family portrait,
the smiles our faces bore
to give our fathers reason.
The old Ford, metal he earned
his face blank for, long ago
compressed to bright
scrap in the yard.
Ashes, son, ashes, daughter.
1924 was a mill yard
and I was its dust,
the arc from there
to the tree you sit under,
my unparalleled splendor,
my pre-flight in a dusk too choked
to see through, my dalliance,
sweethearts, through the last innocent war.
I did what I was told
and I did it my own way.

          * * * *

Luck was a lady
but I knew better.
We were luck,
crammed in the back seat,

landscape our eternity
shifting through the window.
Everyone was as good as us,
but no one knew the lines.
Your love hangs a worm
from a bluebird's beak,
tell me who isn't hungry?
How did you go on giving
all from your own dry mouth,
your sorrowing bread crumb,
my love, yes, my assault,
sprung near the end of the day.

* * * *

If you say a man
is absurd to run
reciting his horror
magnificently each morning
into the judicial mirror,
what will you say to rain?
Will you lift the piano
to prove you didn't fear?
I'm not saying I might not help
you on a given day, but usually
I don't muster that particular
kind of stamina.
His noise is my life's sentence.

* * * *

Here. Stalin's son couldn't stand his luck,
his father's or his own, no matter.
Maybe the electric fence
was buzzing a lullaby
ooh ah ooh ah ooh ah
a croon so deep in his chest
all he had to do was

* * * *

Your father's driving in a circle
with his head on his chest
and mother doesn't seem to notice.
You're telling her over and over
again to *look* but it's your dream,
not mine. I'm trying to speak to you,
not to myself. I'm waiting by a break
in the fence for someone
to walk the pond with,
but tonight I'm unusually worried.
I want the evening to let up.
I want to keep talking
and urge the huge trout,
so algae-riden they must
have been eating this pond
for years, to keep flipping
their dull silver into the air.
Every clumsy thud serves, somehow,
an edict against the thriving yellow
grass the wind blows through
with no sound. It doesn't matter
that no place remains familiar.
If I keep talking,
even here could be home.
There are lives I walk into
through a slight change in tone.
I don't think you'd call me a liar.
With nothing but desire to own,
a farmer with knee-high boots
and a three-legged dog limping down
the gravel road takes on a semblance
of me, or you. You might think
he'll shoot me, but I'm a woman,
a girl to him probably, mostly grown

anyway and nervously at ease.
Of course I can't say but
I think it'd all be the same
if I was a man or a boy.
Belonging implies possession
and the days I don't notice
even the echoing din of a garbage truck,
I think you could say I don't exist.

* * * *

My mother's art is not my own.
No snow ever fell that shade of blue
and the yellow light in the cabin window
is a comfort no one's ever owned, have they?
And even if they built it together, and for us,
inside, there were only four walls
to bump into so I ventured out,
stumbling.

* * * *

And came down from the crags
at a different time of day, then,
in another family, with much less talk
and nearly blind in the dark. And still
it was the same *10 minutes, 10 minutes,*
and we'll be there. . . . but where were we
until then . . . evergreen flanking
on both sides, armed in this century's colorful
slash, meant to mark the trail home?

(for Sarah)

ANGEL WING

> This is not my beautiful house.
> —David Byrne

1. The Equator

"Our last wars were written
by no one. We heard tell
of a faceless enemy dropping
from trees, took cover
when the language of our dreams
slurred to a hymnal of static.
Who could bleed freely
in the context?
Oh, our limbs shattered
like any historical men, but we
were not men. Rather,
it was a drowning we endured,
the blood that refused to leave
the body mocking those distinctions
one by one, 'not a man, not
a woman, not a nation, not
a rat, drowning is death
by water in any language,
I'll give you my word
on that.' Terrible carnage.
We lived moving toward
what we could not see
and died without a landmark
to place our hate."

2. Cape Fear: a Digression in Two Voices Speaking at Once

Of course we had to
kill the author
moving as we were always towards

    (and the heart of the
      hissing drums)

each other wasn't that
the point   Come in what is out
there come in from the body
of rain

    (the water that is my face
      who dare keep me from thy
      water)

Our prayers guiding the light
in the guard tower

    (thoult come no more
      never never never
      never, etc.)

the tower the thing
that kept us true

    (beauty an open mouth on
      the water)

Albeit pity could exist
in the closing of their eyes

    (the whirlpool that cannot
      will not)

mein guard mein watched
the light the knife
you can't feel as it enters

    (sing willow nor raise you
      from the dead)

3. Angel Wing (Icarus Arrives)

O and see how you flicker so boldly
father far now away from the terrible
charity of clouds. It burns far truer
than ever you promised. It was worth it

wasn't it, dying the first time, for this?
Those birds' bodies had souls I couldn't squeeze
from their dry little mouths. I heard them
speaking sadly as we fell from the sky.

Here where the lie of atmosphere expires
little feathers, I whisper *I love*
my eyes no longer the glass you plead through.
Is this the blank gaze father is this the end

of desire there was something I wanted
to remember before we pass there was

TO MY TEACHER

There's no one to tell this day's freedom,
a magpie shirring repeatedly,
        it has to be good enough,

into thin air, pine tree's shadow
trembling (this shaking I
        witness), trembling on a curtain's

sheer cloth. I say *today is a day
for the father* and do you hear,
        dear, as yet unnamed

shadow? Here is the texture
of his indecision. A back
        to an Oklahoma sun, a gun

in hand, an animal to be killed,
to be spared. Where do you think this
        is? A secret non place where you,

unholy listener, may attach your own
names? Corn in neat rows behind him
        casting an obligatory shadow

over the rose garden, thorns
in place in the red and yellow,
        the looking of those he called

children. Was it pain he felt?
I could say I feel the metal
        of the gun he borrowed, hear

the moans of the animal but. No answer
to who put us here *listening* (and the stones
        will bear the wind's language

until they are ash) clenched with a gun
(because its retort signifies an end
let us hear it)
        we don't know how to use in his hand

the animal springing with each badly placed bullet
the body defying logic with every
sudden pulse when please it's dead
        changing the rhetorical *end*

                * * * *

This is a place we will never inhabit
        wanting to be true, my father
        only a need speaking through

        this shaking, die damn you die.
        The animal, a small, white cat
unlucky enough to be under the lawn mower,

spirit revealed, the present, *oh seething
        life* my mother whispered *don't look*
        through. Rooms I've lived in,

        bodies I've climbed, curtains peeled
        back to the courtesies of different
human scenes, a doll's head in the gutter,

glass green eyes open, implores a return.
        Where am I supposed to go, living
        as I do by an animal's precedent?

        Into a litany of broken glass?
        Who will wash me with their tongue?
All childhood a finally dead cat.

                * * * *

In the middle of *something,*
riffed with dog barks and the rational
hammer nailing, a magpie sings. *Something*

from this grounded, dust filled view,
strapping all of it down at the edges,
the magpie singing from an instinct both

predatory and famished, not a twig
unturned that doesn't belong to the invisible.
This hammering just grows louder, dear blow

—hard act of faith, erecting yet another
scaffold to place under the hand of this
great unseen. What is it that our spirit

has in common, father, hammer, white cat,
magpie, writhing as we do beneath *something*
that has its hands in our genitals, in our

private parts, as if we owned anything
but the desire it created in the body. White cat,
magpie, skirt incensed, the rubble of our discordant—

oh vowel, oh nail—periphery. It is not love
this thing that pushes us here. It is not love
but an empty space—here's a little dirt

and part of it's yours—asking
to be filled. It's not love but a gaping
zero added to the petroglyphs, the signatures,

(will you meet me at the river) this nothing
that is not love but reflects its motion,
prescribed. You are not born yet who could know

this, *see how it is nought without
you,* a small place, attendant, but as yet,
wholly free of fire.

THE POSSIBILITY OF ANOTHER WORLD

Because I'm crawling in it now
out here in the field, wind
an amazing animal I need
to imitate. Without its motion
I am only crippled beyond
a doubt, no matter the beautiful question
I may raise, spread here
in someone's golden hair. Overhead,
the startled, white last gasp
breaths some other worldly bird
mutters—sometimes I wish
I could put my teeth into that foreign
sound but I'm reminded
of these lovers I saw once
on a park bench—
how I wanted to be them
but for the indefinite form
they melded in the otherwise
distinctly ornamental green.
They were on the red bench
by three monumental cannons
and they were blending, I swear,
into one brown smear,
clumsy, you know, as if their limbs
were stitched together
but they had forgotten to give up
or divide control. I could see
they were lost; she used his leg
for an arm, and most of his face,
his expression, dear god,
smothered in the fold of her lap.
But—and this is why I'm choking now
so appalled am I at this remembered
picture's lack of perspective—
when they stood up!

What an agony of separation
            they grew into,
standing there embarrassed, rigid
            and quite independent
of anything at all. They stood, as it were,
            formally correct, in the day's
revelation of rust completing the trees
            above them, cars insisting
in the surrounding square, even a dog
            raised in a kind of unity
over the flower urn. It was utter,
            their loneliness. The cannons'
barrels were plugged, I noticed, and a man
            looked at me in my usual
curve on the grass. I felt it then, how I was meant
            to dot the surface even when
I'd left the picture. There where the sun
            splits the grass to its single
spirit, I am pulling, ranging to divine
            the whole distance
from me to the impossible lovers—
            the wind blows through the grass—
my fidelity to this home,
            the one I'm talking in now.

SPRING

To stand here and not want to be part of it,
ever. That's what he said. In the darkened
room, to love the long curtain
for what it keeps in, long trials
of father and son, the broken down
stairs that he became heir
to. Speechless. To miss the slow walk

through the graveyard and the child's
grave written in the ordinary
marbles, marbles rolled on a green day,
most likely, as today. The young,
indistinguishable name engraved
with multi-colored balls, all the reds,
blues, yellows taking on a final
easily sought formality in the spring's
filtered light; to miss the final flap
of the common cardinal, the one who stayed
all winter. That's what it means to be alone.
He only made me sorry.

And aware of what I was missing there.
The white intelligence someone chose to give
the grave rows, and the crisscross path I felt
my way on, uninterpreted. So that the grass growing
even on a newly dug grave became a promise
of the promises given back in full, in twice as
full. Or, it was only the day, the burn of the sun
on my face, my unheld hands parting the brambles
to find my way out of the graveyard and onto
the ordinary street again, watching some kids
play follow-the-leader and then the five city blocks
I made a square of and found myself home.

ARS POETICA

I will go home
when my mother dies,
finger her jewlery, drape
her many scarves round
and round my head,
pack the last
of her smell into boxes.
Her cupid lamps
I will sell, her paintings
burn. I will not find any letters.

The glass animals
gazing serenely from my kitchen sill
shatter one by one.
Upon waking,
the sun grazes
my face.
The dust in the air
blazes into sight.
I raise her lips to my cup.
I ask the day to keep me.

FREEFALL

> . . . mother, the world is too much with me.
> —from *Casper Hauser* or *One Man Against*
> *the World and God Against Them All.*
>
> The first casualty of war is innocence.
> —from *Platoon*

This soft white flare
arcing over the dense, post-hell
jungle, from the aerial,
twice-removed view,
dots chinese lanterns or fireflies,
evening just to come to a party
in the tropics. I'm trying
to see what's not there,
trying to see how it would fit—
the son of man bellying,
named for the narrow tunnel
always in the dim light,
groping into the tokens
of our love for him—
a table, two chairs,
a dead man in a hammock.
Something in this looking
has to narrow, focus hard
through a foliage so thick
I feel what it's like
to beat someone's head in,
marvelling in how it all comes apart
so neatly. This is not Casper Hauser's
cauliflower brain, the autopsy
revealing in the flare of such starkly
clinical light, the irregular curves
reminiscent of the forgiving nature
of the desert—how easily these tracings

are lost there, the sand freeing
the caravan from a mercenary journey,
sinking back into itself, not a soul
left accountable erased
as they are in the freefall,
from whole chapters determining *cause*
in distinctly nomad wars—
This war torn brain finally
only formally, for lack of a better
word, correct, the pieces flying
in a slow motion spray,
the blood and flesh a rainbow
with nothing but more of the same
at the end. I was trying to say
I can see how we live in both
their bodies—father, child of god—
but I find I live in neither
and stand compelled to watch
silently the man running scatter shot
into the air of the waiting jungle.

TOWARDS

It was love
and then it was poetry
but it was poetry
that believed in love.
It was doubt and then
well, it was faith
but it was poetry
we worried the beads of.
It was life and then
—or before then?
in the actual face of,
in the deep pilings of,
fallen in the bagged old city of—
and then it was life—
savaged in the mouthings,
scraped in the garbage tin
of, eaten in the holy, oh holy day of—
it was life, but it was poetry
we closed her lids with.